Surrounded by the Energy of Angels

HOUSE of ORBS

CECILIA CZEKANOWICZ

Copyright © 2020 by Cecilia Czekanowicz

All rights reserved. No part of this publication may be reproduced, distributed, or transmitted in any form or by any means, including photocopying, recording, or other electronic or mechanical methods, without prior written permission of the publisher, except in the case of brief quotations embodied in critical reviews and certain other noncommercial uses permitted by copyright law. For permission requests, write to the publisher, addressed "Attention: Permissions Coordinator," at the address below.

ARPress
45 Dan Road Suite 36
Canton MA 02021

Hotline: 1(800) 220-7660
Fax: 1(855) 752-6001

Ordering Information:
Quantity Sales. Special discounts are available on quantity purchases by corporations, associations, and others. For details, contact the publisher at the address above.

Printed in the United States of America.

ISBN-13   Paperback   979-8-89389-719-7
                    eBook   979-8-89389-720-3

Library of Congress Control Number: 2024922190

DEDICATION & ACKNOWLEDGEMENTS

This is book is dedicated to the people that have helped and supported me throughout my life.

I would like to acknowledge the following people in particular:
My beautiful husband John, thank you so much for the support, love and belief in me always.
I would like to thank my dearest parents for their love and care.

Thank you to the angel orbs that constantly support and guide me. Thank you for choosing me to be the one to share your brilliance and beauty with the world.

Thank you to Sue Kennedy and Lou Reed from The Creative HQ for helping me get this book off the ground, for your continual guidance, support, patience, love and care.

TABLE OF CONTENTS

INTRODUCTION

One of the first experiences I had with orbs was on a lovely summer's evening in 2013. I had a real urge to go outside and look at the night sky. To my surprise, I saw a red orb exploding before my eyes, I raced back inside and told my husband how excited I felt as this was the start of a whole new beginning of the angelic realm. I remember thinking *'why me?'* I didn't understand.

(;ping back as far as 2010, I do remember this energy that I had felt running through my body, it was like a surging electric energy, I dismissed that feeling as this powerful rush of energy was coming to me at the most unexpected moments. I didn't know how to deal with this sensation, my thoughts were to find a quiet place and release this powerful surge of energy. This is what I did, and I kept it to myself and didn't want anyone else to know as I am a private person. This surging energy was coming to me each day.

I did know however that this was something special to me and this feeling was building in me more and more. I kept saying to myself 'Why me?" I am a grandmother who loves gardening and doing her own thing, enjoying life and I have been blessed to have been chosen by the angelic realm.

I remember this particular day in Autumn at Blackheath, it was 10am and the liquid ambers were looking amazing, there were people buzzing around and I was standing behind a table with my husband selling wares at the local markets. I remember saying to my husband that I needed a break. I felt an urgent need to release my energy. I just stood there and this amazing energy was all over me, consuming me, I thought *'Gee, what is this?"*

I felt frightened at first about what this heavy electric energy was, it was so powerful. I raised my arms up to release the energy and after it subsided I headed back to my husband. He wondered why I had taken so long.

An hour had passed and I felt this energy sensation again. I went for another walk as I needed to release the energy once again. I knew something was happening to me, however, I still felt scared and I didn't want anybody to know about what was happening to me. This happened about 5 times during the day.

I kept it to myself as I felt too embarrassed to mention it to my husband until I completely understood what was happening to me.

The days went by and I kept it to myself and didn't say anything. I was beginning to understand what was going on however I chose to keep it to myself. These were my own private thoughts where there was a sense of excitement in me and my confidence was starting to build up.

The time had finally arrived where I had the courage to tell my husband why I needed to keep taking breaks that day at Blackheath. I explained to him that I was getting all this energy through me and I needed to release it. His response was that I had been chosen. I felt very shocked when he said that and I thought "WOW", my confidence grew and I felt completely excited. A part of me was still questioning it asking "why me?"

I am a person that simply loves being in my backyard and to this day I still get surges of energy and I love it.

Communicating with the Orbs

My ego gets in the w a y sometimes when the orbs are trying to communicate with me. Sometimes I feel vulnerable and scared when this happens, so I find a quiet place (usually in my backyard) and I surrender to the beautiful power of the energy.

I lay still or sit and go into a trance, it's a beautiful space for me, it's my aura in which the orbs penetrate me, my ego is in the way as I am writing this. They communicate with me by sight as well, this is how they give me power, it is what happened in Blackheath that day as well as when my mother was sick, they were there to guide and protect me all at the same time.

I wasn't coping well, so they gave me another direction to choose (which I didn't like) they presented me with my inner child. I didn't want to look at that, they told me to work at my inner child, as I wasn't doing this at all.

I could feel their presence and energy as they took over my inner child, it made me feel it was right at that moment in time. I have since done a lot of work around my inner child through metaphysics and personal development courses. My orbs are still with me communicating and giving me positive direction.

I've come a long way in life and feel very blessed that the orbs have chosen me, so I now allow them to communicate with me whenever they need to. When I know they are trying to communicate, I sink low into my body and allow them to communicate what they need me to know.

How the orbs guide me

I am getting stronger energy now At times, I am in the middle of doing something like house work and the orbs let me know. That is when I stop what I am doing and go outside and take pictures, this can happen day or night.

The experience is beautiful and I know that there is a higher source that is wanting me to spread the love of life. I see the orbs every day and night, they have no concept of time.

When I take pictures of these pulsating orbs I can see them in detail and they show me very interesting things that I know they want me to see.

Did you know that orbs come with auras? Their message to me is to trust in what they are showing and telling me, start using it the way they are telling me, this is why I am writing this book, it's to show the world that there is love and hope in the angelic realm, look at the sky and listen to what's been said!

Love and light,
Cecilia
xx.

Orbs are still a mystery to many people. I know it was all new to me until my first encounter with them. I decided to find out more so I could understand what was going on so I could explain it to others in this book.

Orbs are best described as spheres of light that are white in colour, however they also show up as different colours which I will explain in more detail later in this book.

Orbs are mainly seen at night as this is their natural environment. Orbs show up in digital photographs as transparent balls of light and many people see them with their own eyes, they are beautiful amazing spheres of lights that represent the presence of angels surrounding you.

These balls of light can appear in a variety of different shapes, sizes, and colours. They have been captured by people indoors, outdoors, in homes, churches, schools, construction sites, burial grounds, and more. Videos of orbs are becoming more common; they show as light anomalies moving across the frame. The orbs appear as circular lights that either float or move, and at times travel at a very high rate of speed.

Angels travel to our earthly dimension through these light rays and at times use orbs as their vehicle for their energy to travel within.

Let's take a closer look at what angel orbs are and what they mean:

Orbs are electromagnetic energy fields that contain angelic energy, to humans they appear as a form of light. As mentioned, angels use the orbs as their vehicle to travel, just like you and I use a car to travel from one place to another.

Orbs do not have corners to restrict their energy flow, this way they can be efficient spirit vehicles. The circular shapes orbs represent eternity, wholeness, and unity spiritually, these are all concepts that relate directly to the angelic missions.

Angel orbs travel through the universe at a higher vibrational frequency than us humans can even begin to perceive. However, once they reach the person whom God has called them to help, they slow down long enough to be detected by the intended person.

Not all orbs represent a spirit, some are simply particles that reflect light and nothing more.

Angel orbs are so much more than a simple ball of light; they are very complex. When you view one closely, you will see intricate patterns of geometric shapes that also have colours that divulge the different characteristics held within the auras of the angels who are traveling within them.

Most spirit orbs contain the energy of holy angels; however, some may contain the energy of fallen angels from the evil side of the spiritual realm. Therefore, it's important to always test and identify the spirits you come across and protect yourself from danger.

Holy angels radiate feelings of love, joy, and peace. If you feel afraid or upset in the presence of an orb, this is a sure sign that the spirit inside is not one of God's holy angels.

House of Orbs

It is more common to see a white orb than a coloured one and this makes sense because guardian angels travel within the white orbs. Guardian angels are present with people more than any other type of angel.

If a guardian angel appears inside an orb, it usually means encouragement and letting you know that you are loved and cared for, or it may simply be to inspire you to have faith especially when you are going through challenging circumstances.

In most instances when angels manifest in orbs, they don't have complex messages to deliver. By them showing up in an orb is a simple and unimposing way of blessing the person that sees them.

Seeing an orb is a sign that the person or people are blessed with the goodness, positive energy, and protection of angels. When orbs appear in a location, it is a sign that the angels are hovering and that this location is particularly blessed.

Following is a brief description about the colours of orbs, later in the book, we look at the colours and their meanings in more detail.

There are times you will see angel orbs featuring colours, these colours indicate the type of energy that is present within that orb. The meaning of these colours in orbs in most cases corresponds to the meanings of different angel light ray colours that are:

- Blue–power, protection, faith, courage, and strength
- Yellow–wisdom for decisions
- Pink–love and peace
- White–the purity and harmony of holiness
- Green–healing and prosperity
- Red–wise service
- Purple–mercy and transformation

Orbs may also feature colours beyond the seven angel light rays that are associated with other meanings like the following:

- Silver–a spiritual message
- Gold–unconditional love
- Black — shadow
- Brown — danger
- Orange–forgiveness

At times, people can see the faces of spirits within the angel orbs. These faces reveal clues to the emotional messages that the angels are expressing to us.

It does not matter whether orbs are moving fast, slow or standing still, they are spiritually intriguing. Orbs are known to 'hang around' people, the belief is that orbs are angels, spirit guides or deceased relatives.

I can attest to this as I am surrounded by them wherever I go, and they definitely surround my home as you can see from the photos in this book.

On a beautiful spring morning in November of 2014, I ventured outside feeling free and full of hope. I felt very blissful and inspired to take a picture this particular morning. As you can see the results were amazing, I felt completely blessed by what I saw. The angels had rewarded me with this beautiful picture of orbs surrounding the bright sun.

Our garden is <u>filled</u> with many beautiful trees, bushes and plants.
In particular, our beautiful bottle brush is so vibrant and very pretty,
it is one of my favorites.
I love the great outdoors,
it heals my soul and I just love how the orbs have embraced my bottle brush,
I hope you like it too!

It is a wonderful feeling being able to walk outside in my backyard barefoot,
there is no better way to enjoy nature at its best! Wondering around my backyard on this
day, I looked up into the sky to look at the amazing shape the clouds had formed,
at times I have even seen faces.

Outside in my backyard is our veggie patch amongst the beautiful nature that surrounds us. As you can see here, a beautiful coloured orb shines bright, you can see here how it has orange and red in it, these orbs really love nature.

This particular orb is letting us know that they are here and to simply trust.

This picture was taken at home in our kitchen, it made me feel blissful and these beautiful orbs want to be shared with the world, so I have created this beautiful book so that you can see how loving they are and to let you know that there is no need to be afraid

These orbs are very powerful with a lot of energy, they are showing me directly that thy are here. When I first took this photo, I was a bit afraid, however, it showed me that there was more to come, not to be afraid and to just keep taking photos.

PULSATING ORB

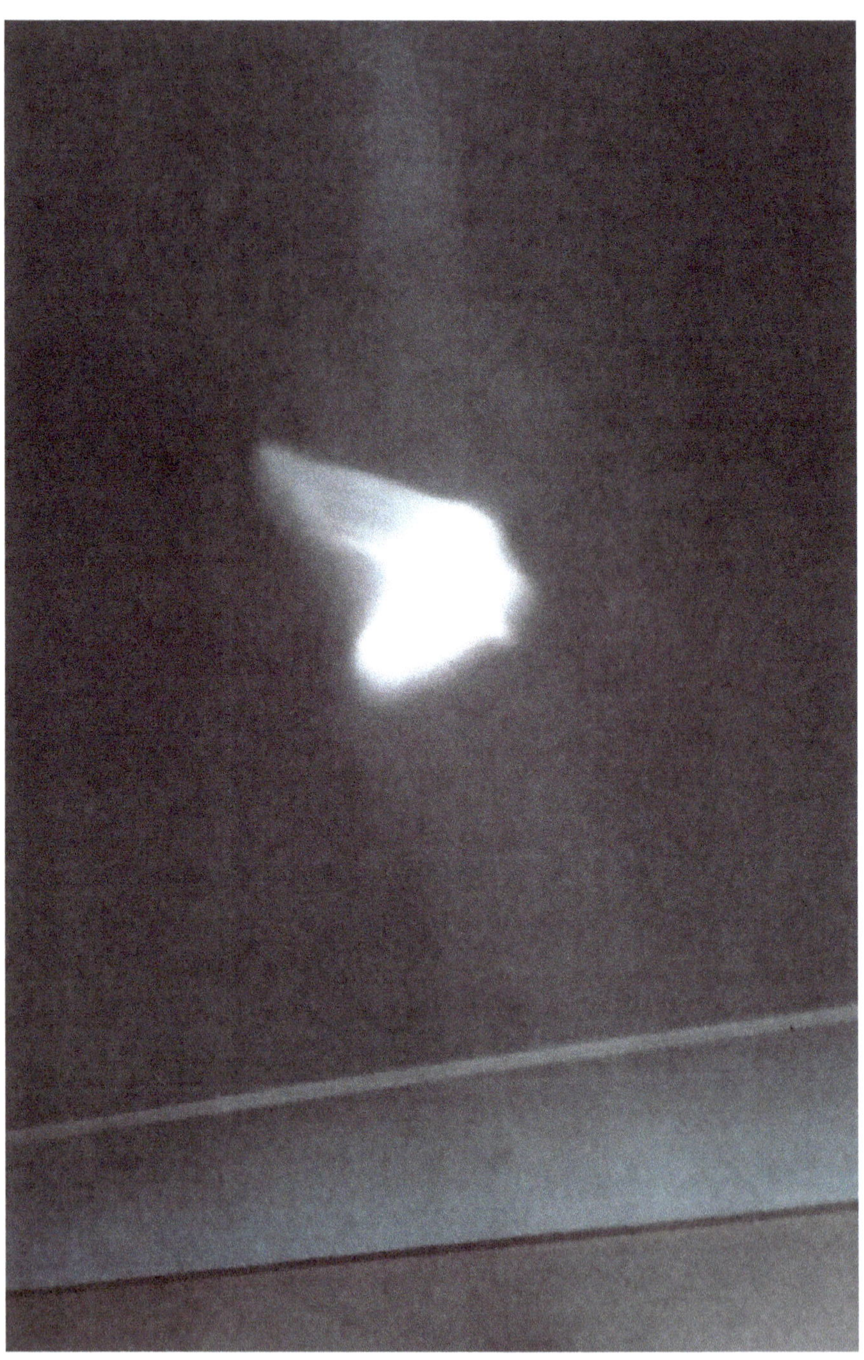

A subtle little angel has come to me giving me power and saying don't be afraid.

This beautiful red energy on the ceiling surrounds the beautiful white orb.
It makes me feel loved and invigorated. I feel truly blessed as these orbs continually show up
in my house in all different areas and rooms of the house.

This is a beautiful orb that greets me quite regularly. This particular one changes its shape to be noticed and I am always drawn into the powerful energy it holds.

ORBS CAPTURED ON VIDEO

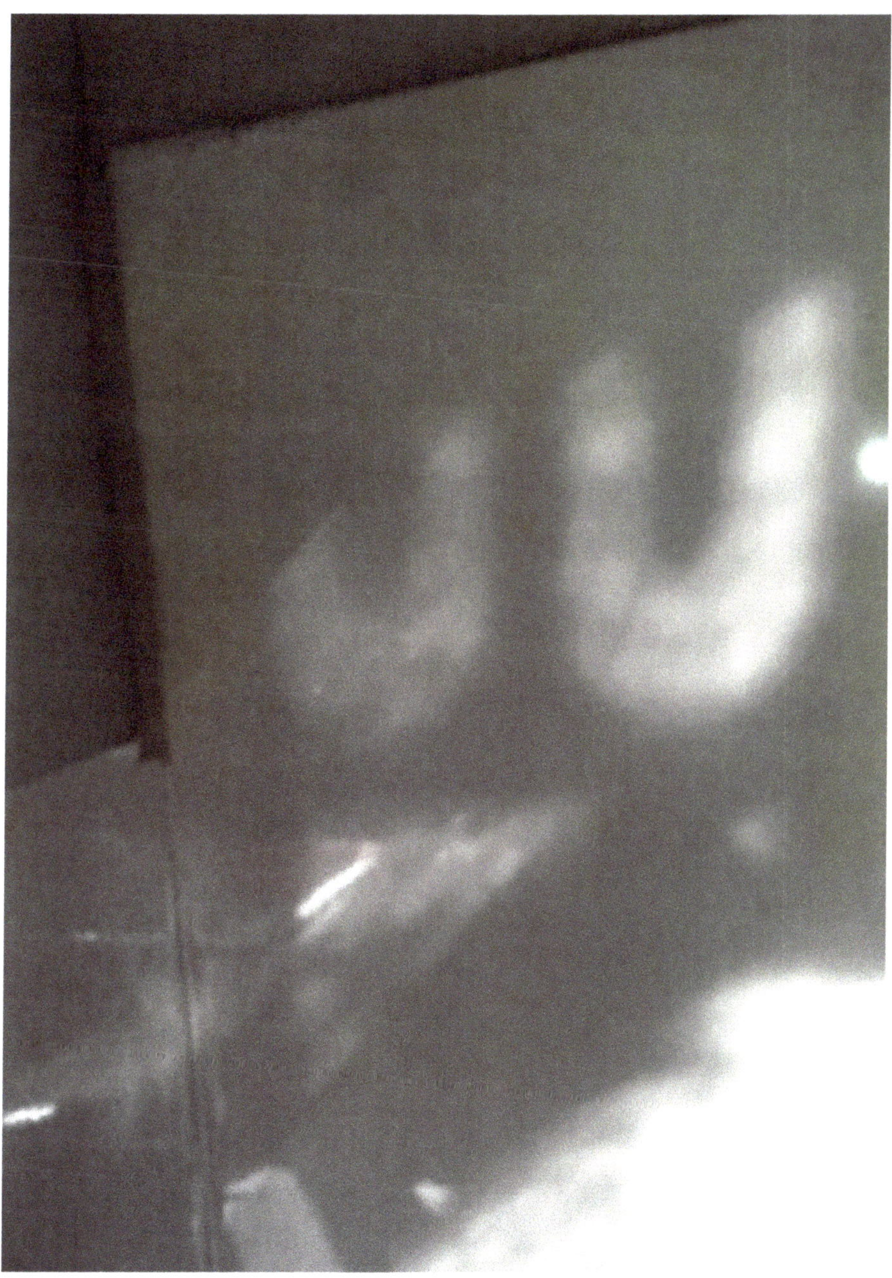

The pulsating letters of J and U can be seen in this video.
To view please visit: https://youtu.be/TrMzthWo510

This video shows how the orbs move around inside of my house.
To view please visit: https://youtu.be/K9U-jvIzm3Y

The orb in this video allows me to feel the energy strongly where it takes me to a higher place, I feel so very blessed.

To view please visit: https://youtu.be/RVx8aZBN0z1

This video shows the beautiful emerald green orb pulsating.
To view please visit: https://youtu.be/WBNZ-marvGA

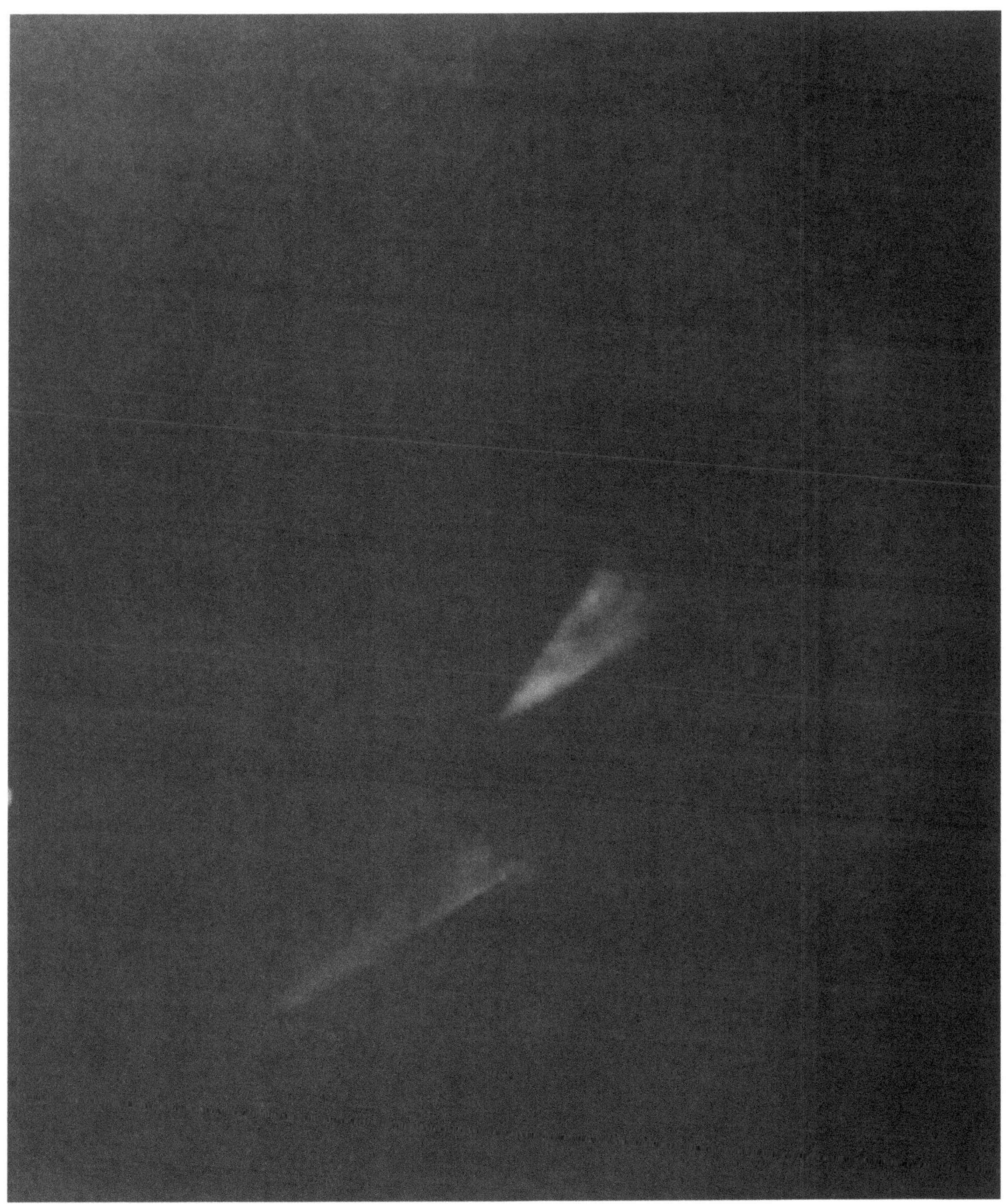

This video shows how the orbs show up on our walls.
To view please visit: https://youtu.be/wSOTOah6eN4

This amazing video shows how the orbs show themselves from the television screen.
To view please visit: https://youtu.be/VoW wtzriUg

This video shows the orbs from the television screen at a different distance.
To view please visit: https://youtu.be/YmqMyzcqLvc

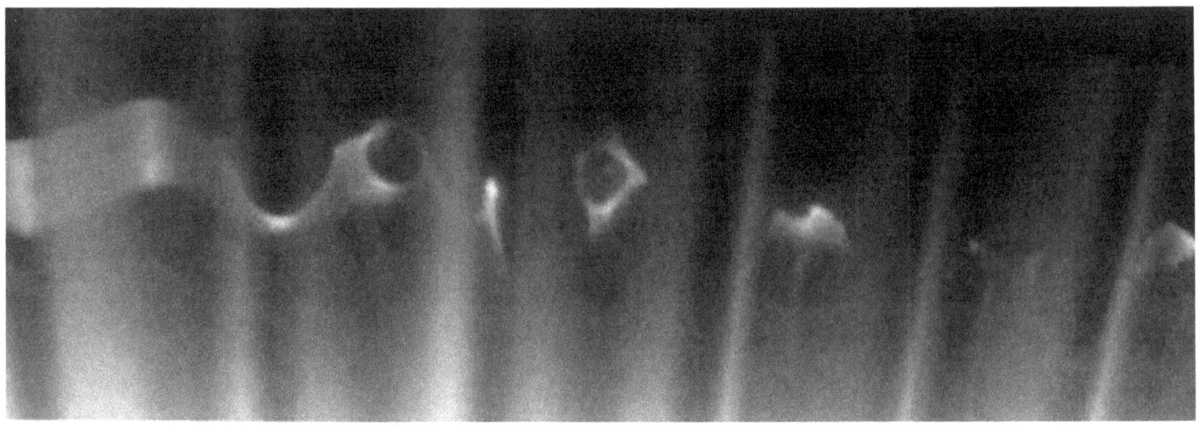

I was cleaning our carport and this pulsating orb energy caught my eye. it was very powerful; these orb energies are with me all the time protecting and loving me.

To view please visit: https://youtu.be/qx5uBJblt5c

We all need space like this branch, it's happy to be alone and free.
This branch stands out so strong, it's not carrying any weight in life!

I am surrounded by love, this is a beautiful green that is love and healing which
I've needed through my life, don't be afraid to love, I am a different person through
the experiences with the orbs and angels.

To be outside for me is of great benefit as it allows me to get peace not only within myself, but with my outer world. Seeing and being in nature in its most natural form is amazing, the added bonus for me is seeing the beautiful orb on the side of this beautiful tree.

Here is another orb in our garden, it brings love to me and power.
I am so blessed with the love of the angels. I continue to take picture of these orbs
as they love to surround us and our home.

With this photo, I was prompted to go outside, my heart was full of love as I took this beautiful picture of this magical orb. Love, love…

These are natural orbs; they give us love and show us the beauty of all the nature that surrounds us. This is a very powerful orb.

This picture is one of my favourites. It is one that is just for me I believe.
I feel so blessed with its subtle mood. I really hope you get as much enjoyment out of it as
I do each time I see this picture.

Every day I am blessed to be receiving beautiful energy around my home and myself.
I am prompted to show people this particular picture.
Please take the time to really look at this image and see the love that emanates from it.

I absolutely love this wonder of nature. Be open to receive this energy as I did when it allowed me to take the picture. The love that these orbs are giving me is so beautiful. Absolutely loving this image and the message it holds for us all.

This picture is a reminder to us all to take time to go outside and be still and to connect
with the orbs. Be open to these beautiful orbs and don't be afraid,
they are here to protect and guide us.

Take time to look at this amazing picture. Relax into it, can you feel the bliss?

These are nature orbs enjoying our front yard.
They are everywhere, it's so easy to surrender to them all.

HOW DO YOU KNOW IF AN ANGEL IS WATCHING OVER YOU?

This is my Guardian Angel!

An enormous comfort to us all is the idea of a guardian angel watching over you.

There are different beliefs around guardian angels, some people believe it is a spiritual being that looks out for their well-being, while other people believe their guardian angel is a deceased loved one who is giving them guidance.

Some people don't quite realise or know when an angel is close by and watching over you. There are a few different signs that can indicate to you when your angel is visiting you.

Look at the following signs to see if any of these have happened to you:

- An angel visit in your dreams — Dreams are considered as the window to your soul, however, they can also indicate to you that your guardian angel is not too far away. They let you know in your dreams that that are watching over you. At times, they may try to deliver a message or simply they are letting you know of their presence

- You may see strange coloured orbs — When you see a bright light or a strange coloured orb, it's not your eyes playing tricks on you, it is more likely the orbs, these lights are said to be the vehicle for angels. These orbs can be seen in your day to day life or in a photograph, these orbs are a sign that your guardian angel is by your side

- A sudden sweet smell from nowhere — When an unexpected sweet smell appears that you cannot explain it is a sign that your guardian angel is nearby. These sweet scents are a way for your guardian angel to reach out to you letting you know they are there with you. Some of the smells could be fragrant flowers, food, or perhaps a perfume that a deceased loved one used to wear

- Finding a white feather — The most common sign from your angels is to see a white feather cross your path in the most unlikely location. It is understood that this happens when you are most in need of knowing that they are there with you, guiding and protecting you

- Your baby or pet sees something you can't see — It is known that the angels put animals and babies at ease. Have you ever seen your baby smiling at something you can't see or perhaps your pet is staring at a certain spot in the room? This is a sure sign that your guardian angel is present

- Seeing the angels in the clouds — Have you ever laid on your back looking up at the sky and the clouds? Looking to see what shapes you can see? These shapes are a sign from your guardian angel and can be different shapes like angels, hearts, or symbols that have a particular meaning to you

- Seeing angel numbers in the most common places — One of the most common ways angels will try to grab your attention and guide you is through angel numbers. These numbers have specific meanings that may be personal to you or they have a spiritual meaning like 444 or 11.11, again it is your guardian angels trying to communicate with you
- When you experience a sudden change in temperature — Just like the sudden sweet smell that appears, another sign from your angels could be in the sudden change in temperature. This could be a sudden chill or it could be a feeling of warmth that surrounds you. This is a sign that your angel is giving you a reassuring hug
- Hearing muffled voices — You may not be able to talk to your angel literally, however, they are always trying to communicate to you in one way or another. When you are in a quiet room and you suddenly hear muffled voices, this is a sign that your angels are trying to communicate with you and letting you know they are there by your side
- The feeling that someone is there with you — You know how you get that feeling that you are not alone, that someone is there with you? This is a sure sign that your guardian angel is there with you in the room
- The feeling of a tingling sensation at the crown of your head — You will notice that you feel a sudden warmth at the crown of your head, it is also understood that it can feel the same as when your foot goes to sleep. The relationship between the crown of your head and an angel's halo is known to be a very powerful connection. This tingling sensation is another way your angel tries to communicate with you

These signs mentioned above are the way your guardian angel lets you know of their presence, they are letting you know that you are not alone and that someone is watching over you.

Angels are a pure spirit created by God. They are the messengers of God. The angels were created for us to call them when needed.

The angels are there for us all the time whenever we need some help. An angel can be called upon for anything you need help with, this can be to help you feel happy, to help you through a rough patch or simply helping you find a car park. The angels always work for the highest good of everyone concerned.

How do you know when an angel is present?

In energetic terms, angels vibrate at a high frequency, they do not have a physical form like us, so therefore they need to communicate to us of their presence in various ways as discussed previously.

Other ways they try to communicate with us is by stroking your face or hair, or you may see flashes of light out of the corner of your eye, or by seeing brightly coloured orbs.

They communicate telepathically with us to get the message across. Their message is always in a soft, loving voice that is not controlling or demanding.

How do you know the difference between angels and spirit guides?

Our guardian angels are assigned to us at birth and they remain with us throughout our lifetime. Angel guides on the other hand are who we call upon when we need that extra bit of help.

We are all able to call upon the angels and our guardian angel to help us in any situation. Their role is to help lead us in the right direction, they are here to reassure and guide us when we ask for their help. Many of us forget to ask for help, so please remember that whenever you need a helping hand...Just ask the angels!

Please remember that they cannot interfere with our life lessons however, they can help make our life's journey a lot easier!

Our guides on the other hand are our best friends in the spirit world. They are there to help you and available immediately as soon as you ask for their help or guidance.

Our guides give us inspiration and pass messages to us through our intuition. We do have one main spirit guide throughout our life plus we have others that come and go as the need arises, this will depend on what lessons are needed to be learnt.

Spirit guides have previously lived in the physical realm where they have gained the knowledge and wisdom throughout all their many lifetimes. On the other hand, angels have never lived life as a human as they vibrate at a different frequency, therefore they can offer us a loving presence that helps protect and guide us.

Angels are only allowed to intervene without being asked is when there is a life-threatening situation that happens. If it is not our time to pass over, then an angelic intervention can help to save our lives.

You will know when an angel wishes to make their presence known, you will have an overwhelming feeling of warmth and love, a sense of security and reassurance will surround you.

The wonderful news is that as well as the angels, you may feel a connection to one or mor of the archangels. These are the higher angels that have greater responsibilities and watch over much larger areas and groups of people, they are known as the over-arching angels, this is where thy got the name "archangels".

Most people are quite familiar with Archangel Michael, Archangel Raphael or even Archangel Gabriel.

It is important to remember that all the archangels are multidimensional beings and can help anyone that calls them for help, they are never too busy to help, are always available and react and respond rather quickly.

Please see below an introduction to some of the other Archangels that are the top eight.

- **Archangel Michael**

  Michael is known as the head of all the archangels, many people have already felt a connection with him and call upon him often. Michael helps with protection (for ourselves, homes, and loved ones), and psychic clearing and protection (this includes cutting cords with his sword). Michael also helps by giving us the courage and strength when we need it, he provides direction and help with our life and life path.

  Michael can be called upon to bring justice to a situation or to help you achieve your personal goals. Michael is the archangel of fire.

  Michael's messages are in most instances very clear and to the point. He is our no-nonsense archangel that we love!

- **Archangel Raphael**

  Raphael is the archangel of healing and healers. You can call upon him when you need help with healing on any level, for yourself or others, even your pets. He is the one you call when you need help developing your healing work. He is the archangel of air. He is often depicted with a pilgrims' staff as he protects those on journeys particularly air travel. He is also the archangel of knowledge and communication and may be called upon to help with improving memory, learning, languages, exams, and business matters.

Raphael is associated with the colour green, and normally appears as a normal looking make of average height. He loves to assist in all aspects of healing.

- **Archangel Gabriel**

  Gabriel is the messenger angel that brings important news and information. Gabriel is associated with a golden light. Gabriel occasionally appears in the female form as Gabrielle. He/she often brings new, unexpected information.

  Gabriel helps in times of hardship or to inspire your imagination and bring your plans to fruition and communication. Gabriel is the archangel of the moon and water. Gabriel is your guide to the inner tides of your subconscious mind. If you are trying to develop your imagination and psychic abilities, then call upon Gabriel to help you.

- **Archangel Uriel**

  Uriel is the fourth of the 'top four' archangels, he is the archangel of peace, both on a personal and global scale.

  Uriel is often a more subtle, gentle being, wise and calming, appearing usually in a golden glow, or as a gentle calming energy or presence that surrounds you. Call upon Uriel to help bring peace to you and your life, or to help bring peace to the world.

  Uriel is the force of spiritual illumination and spiritual passion, magical power and the application of force. He is also known as 'Ariel' and is the archangel of the earth and of peace and salvation.

- **Archangel Chamuel**

  Chamuel is the archangel of love and relationships. It is then no surprise that the colour of Chamuel is pink. Chamuel is kind, loving and sweet, helping us to be more loving and build loving relationships.

Chamuel is known as the heavenly warrior god. Chamuel is ideal to call upon to help you take personal responsibility and develop your self-confidence. Chamuel will also help smooth away any problems you are having in relationships and will help you attract and build more loving and positive relationships.

- **Archangel Jophiel**
  Jophiel is the joyful and uplifting angel. Jophiel helps us to appreciate the beauty of life, nature and assists us with art, music, and creative projects that make our hearts sing.

  Jophiel is associated with the colour yellow and is the archangel of illumination, bringing the light of divine love into the heart of the spiritual seeker. Jophiel is usually depicted with beautiful white wings and helps those that are facing difficult situations.

  Jophiel can be called upon when you need help to feel more joyful, appreciate nature and the beauty of life, will help you bring greater balance and harmony into your life, and will help you with your creative or artistic projects.

- **Archangel Zadkiel**
  Zadkiel is the archangel of teachers, especially those of spiritual teaching and transformation. Zadkiel can help you with knowledge, symbols, new spiritual information, transformation, and help us teach others.

  Zadkiel is associated with the colour purple. Zadkiel uses the purple energy to transform negativity into positive energies. Zadkiel appears as a wise old man with a long white beard with a purple cloak, ancient and wise that is guiding us on the path of enlightenment.

  Zadkiel brings comfort in times of need and lifts the heart. He is the archangel of Jupiter, memory and mercy. His angelic energies can help you attune with divinity and come closer to the pure energies of the cosmos. He influences the way in which you perceive and experience divine inspiration.

- **Archangel Metatron**

  Metatron is said to be the highest of the archangels, the one closest to God. Metatron is the one that watches over and supports all the other archangels. Metatron is a very high and powerful being that normally appears as a large and blindingly bright white light and powerful energy.

  Metatron is the one that provides extra energy and support for those who are looking to do good things in the world. Like Michael, he can provide a powerful energy to help cleanse, protect, assist you, and provides a clear helpful guidance.

These archangels are here to help you. You can call upon them at any time you need help. Next time you need some help, look to see which of these archangels are best suited to help with your problem.

I see a lot of these angel orbs in my front yard,
I take a picture from my window and hey appear.
Look how powerful they are. Just love this image.

This orb is powerful. Trust and be open, don't be afraid, simply surrender to the angel orbs!

I am going to another level in the angelic realm. See how this orb has changed its shape.

I feel enlightenment through seeing this orb. I am opening up.

This orb is an unusual shape that represents Archangel Michael with the green,
he is here to protect us.

The orbs come in many shapes and sizes. This particular orb drew me outside and gave me the message to share with you that they are here to guide us strength and show us love.

As we have discussed, orbs of light or energy orbs can appear either in photographs or to the naked eye. They also appear in many different shapes, sizes and colours.

Most orbs appear as white light, however, some of them can be green, blue, pink, purple, yellow or even multi-coloured.

It is quite common for an orb to display an aura. For example, a white orb may have a green aura, or a red aura etc. It is quite uncommon to see black or grey orbs; however, they do exist.

It is understood that all living beings have an aura that consists of various colours that depicts their personality, their state of mind, trauma, health and so much more. So, if the floating spheres of light are conscious or sentient beings, it could be possible that the orb colours, and the colour of their aura can also represent the same as us when it comes to their personality, emotional state or intention.

Each colour represents an emotion or a state of being as shown in the images below:

Orb Colors and Their Meanings

White to Silver – pure, new, high frequency, protection, strength, power (May apply to Ascended Master, Guardian Angel, Archangel)

Pinks – openness, compassion, affection, love (May apply to Teacher/Guide, Ascended Master, Guardian Angel, Archangel)

Reds – high energy, creative, restlessness, stress, agitation, pain, anger, impending (May apply to Teacher/Guide, Guardian Angel)

Oranges – comfort, healing energy, motivation, hope, strength, courage (May apply to Teacher/Guide, Guardian Angel)

Yellows – pay attention, notice, caution, insight, inspiration, creativity (May apply to Teacher/Guide)

Gold – free flowing energy, tolerance, inspiration, creativity, higher consciousness, wisdom (May apply to Teacher/Guide)

Greens – neutrality, healing, communicative, psychic development (May apply to Teacher/Guide, Ascended Master, Archangel)

Blues – neutrality, tranquility, protection, intuition, strong psychic ability (May apply to Master Teacher/Guide, Guardian Angel)

Purples – at peace, forgiveness, wisdom, psychic & spiritual development (May apply to Master Teacher/Guide, Ascended Master)

Brown to Black – connection to earth, earthbound, immature, underdeveloped, insecure, trapped, tortured, depression, grief, fear

Scarlet Red - Strong willpower, over-inflated ego, pompous, survival oriented, realistic
Dark Red - Anger, pain, psychological impairment
[illegible] - Short-tempered, stress, restlessness
Vermilion (Clear Red) - Creative, powerful, energetic, competitive, passionate
Light Pink - Sensitive, compassionate, affectionate, true love, openness
Salmon Pink - Immature, dishonest
Orange Red - Confident, healing energy
Orange - Strong motivation, healthy, adventurous, courageous, outgoing
Peach - Caring communicator, ability to comfort
Amber - Strong and courageous
Orange-Yellow - Optimistic, scientific, intelligent, perfectionist
Pale Yellow - Shyness, optimistic, hopeful
Lemon Yellow - Strength of direction, fearful of loss
Yellow - Caution, warning
Buttercup - Focused on a course of action (determined), inspired
Mustard - Manipulative, overly analytical, making up for lost time
Gold- Higher level of consciousness, wise, protective, enlightened, tolerance, free-flowing energy
Apple Green - Friendly, communicative
Yellow-Green - Liar, cheater, dishonesty
Olive Green - Miserly, Scrooge-like
Emerald Green - Healer, teacher, love-centered person, fertility
[illegible] - Jealous, low self-esteem, overly sensitive
Turquoise - Therapist, communicative, sensitive, amusement, neutrality
Sky Blue (Light)
Pilot Light Blue - Shielding, protective
Cobalt Blue - Intuitive in a higher dimension
[illegible] - Knows their chosen path, generous, highly spiritual
[illegible] - Shyness, slow yet safe and sure, fearful of truth or being one's self, survival instinct
Indigo - Strong psychic ability, intuitive, deep-feeling
Lavender - Daydreamer, visionary, spiritual peacefulness
Violet - Sensitive, wise, intuitive, idealistic, seeking spirituality
[illegible] - Laziness
[illegible] - Stored information
[illegible] - Humble
White - Pure, transcendent, often a new un-designated energy, high frequency, protective, shielding
Silver - Linked to spiritual realm, spiritual and physical abundance, nurturing, telekinetic energy
Gray - Feeling trapped
Payne's Gray - Depressed, fearful
[illegible] - Tortured, abused, unreleased grief
Raw Sienna - Poor thinking processes, insecure, stressed
[illegible] - Environmentalist, common sense, connected to the earth

ALL ABOUT ORBS IN5D.COM

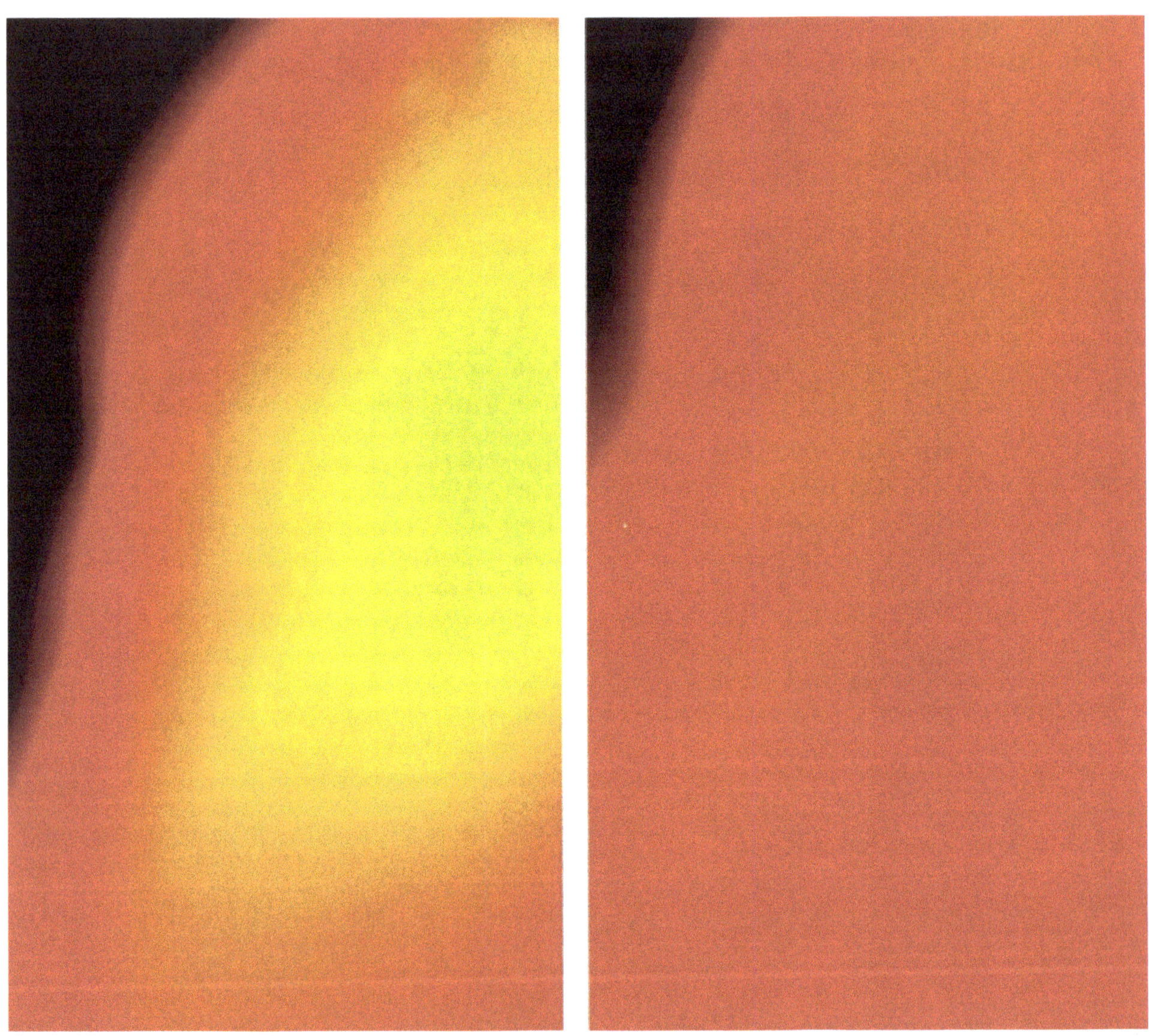

A beautiful sight with colour. There's energy in my backyard. This is my geranium flower

I took this outside another shape and another colour there is divine energy here,
you just need to trust.

This is beautiful, a subtle orb with a beautiful energy that surrounds the orb.

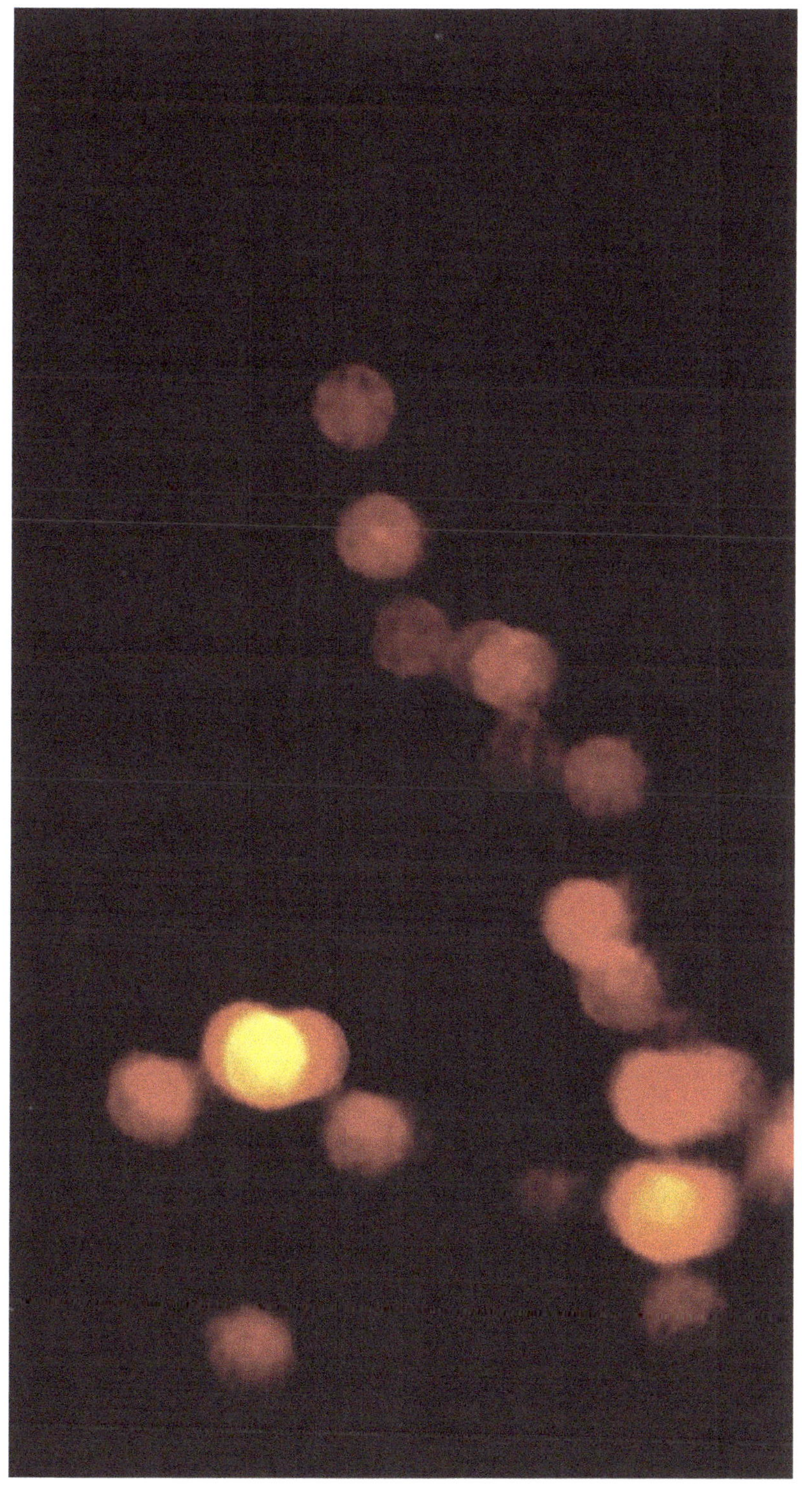

Beautiful orange, red and yellow orbs. I have embraced this love
I am receiving from the angelic realm.

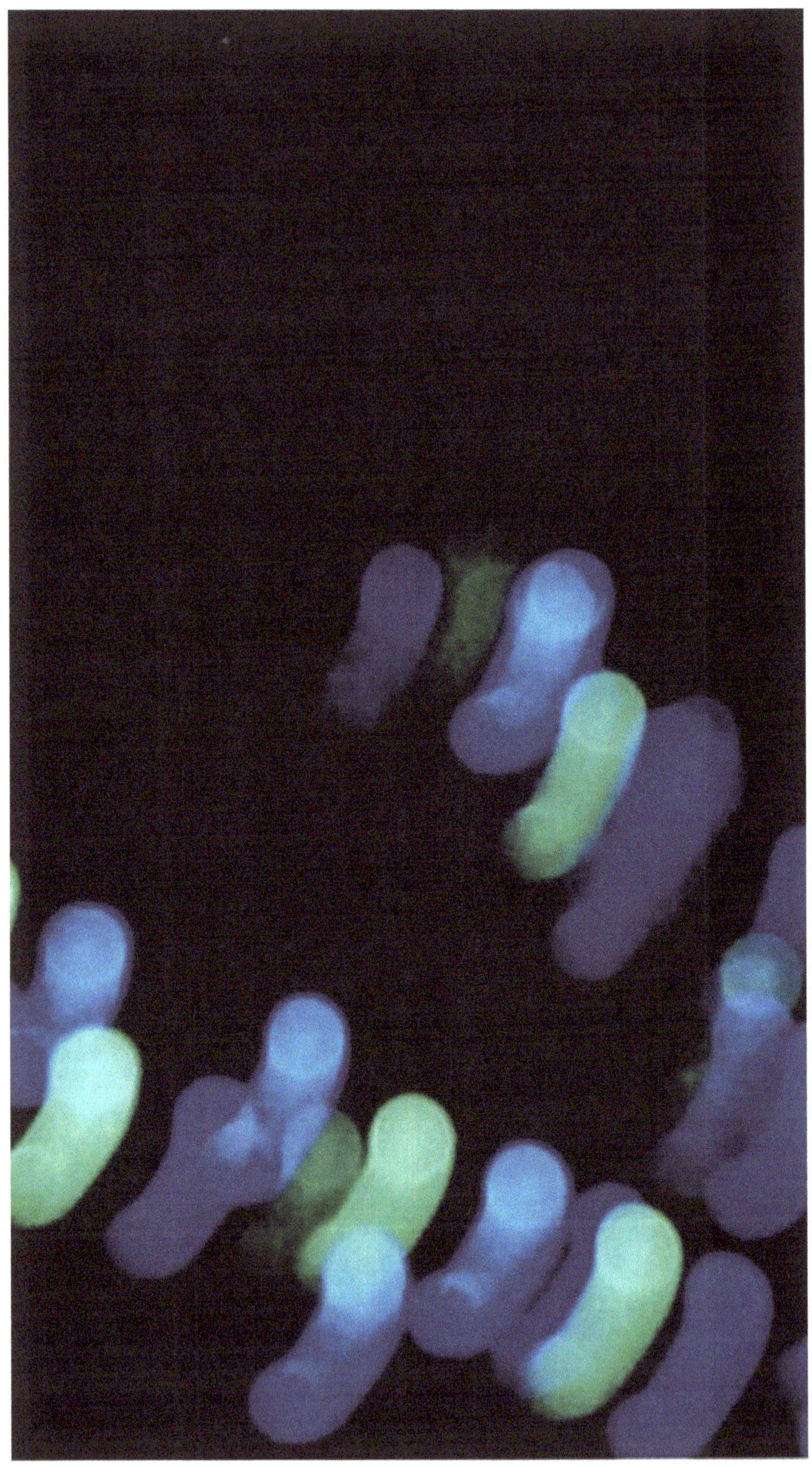

These colours are beautiful, our yard is full of orbs so I trust in what I see, I simply love it!

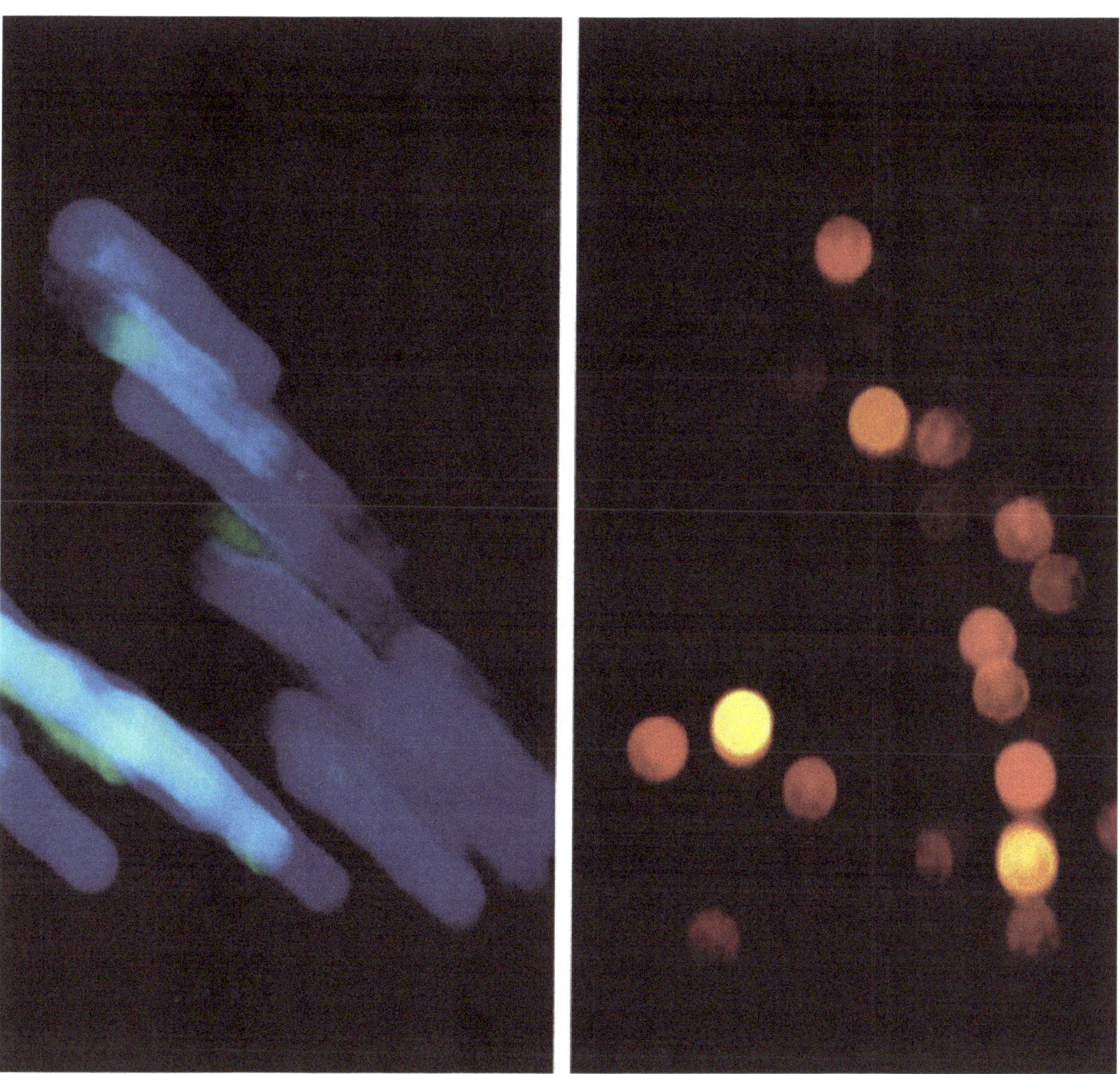

A beautiful Blue Mountains night, the beauty in the stillness, here they are sending us love and light.

This is an orb by night. The angels love us; all you need to do is look around.

This image represents the angels sending love to the world.
If you look closely, you will see a floating heart.

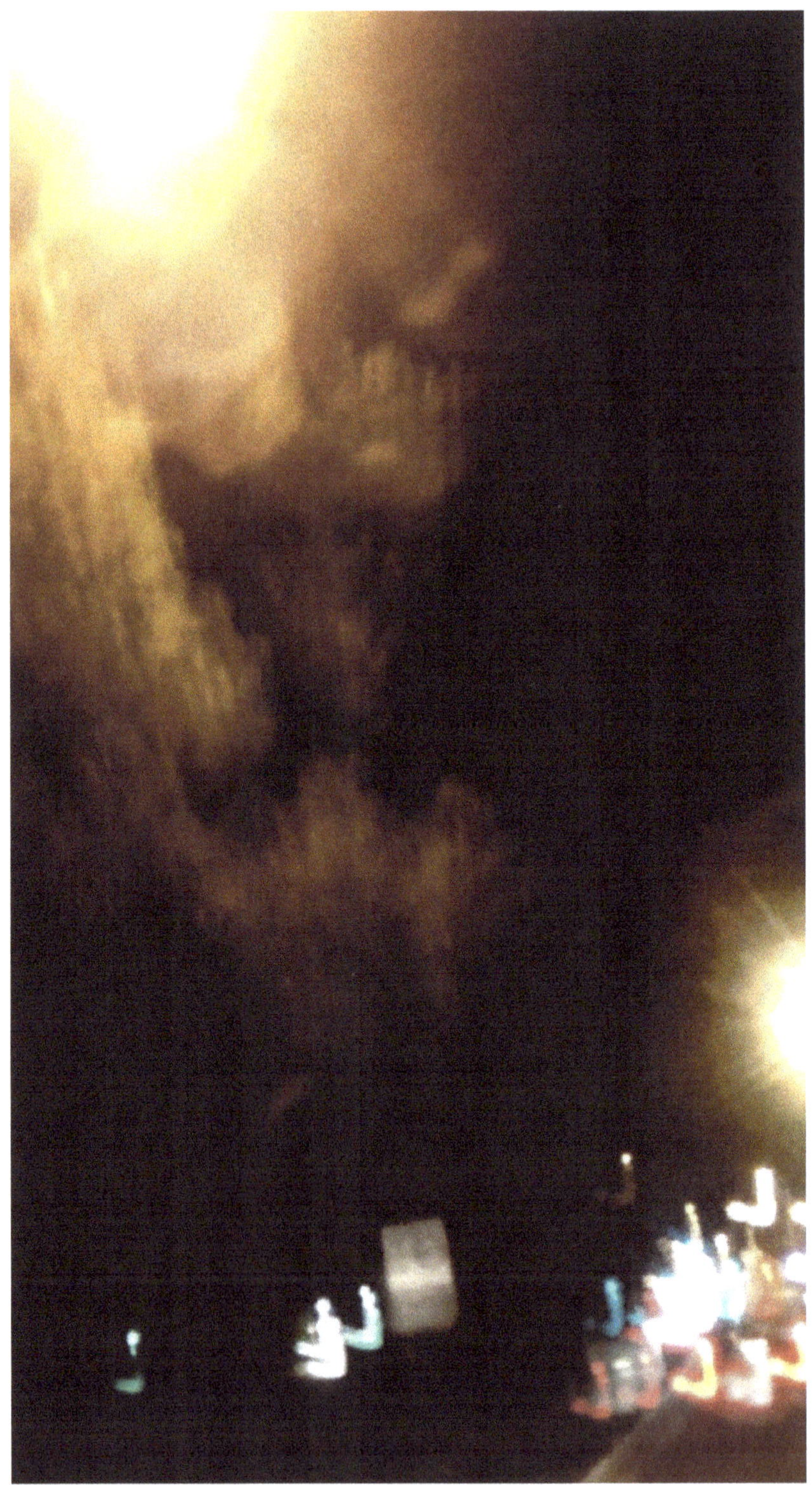

Can you see the letter "L?" The angels want us to love and this image is sending us a strong message showing us the presence of the letter L for love.

This image shows me that these are our friends and they are with us, feel their energy and don't be afraid. I can see a letter in this picture, if you look closely you might see it as well.

In this image I can see a number '2'. The angels are saying "believe and have the hope, the outcome will be positive, all you need to do is ask"

This image shows the floating energy that is so mystical and beautiful all at the same time.

Here I am receiving energy and love, as you can see the letter "L" is clear, I am so blessed –
I want to show you and hope that you enjoy my pictures and allow yourself to be open to
them.

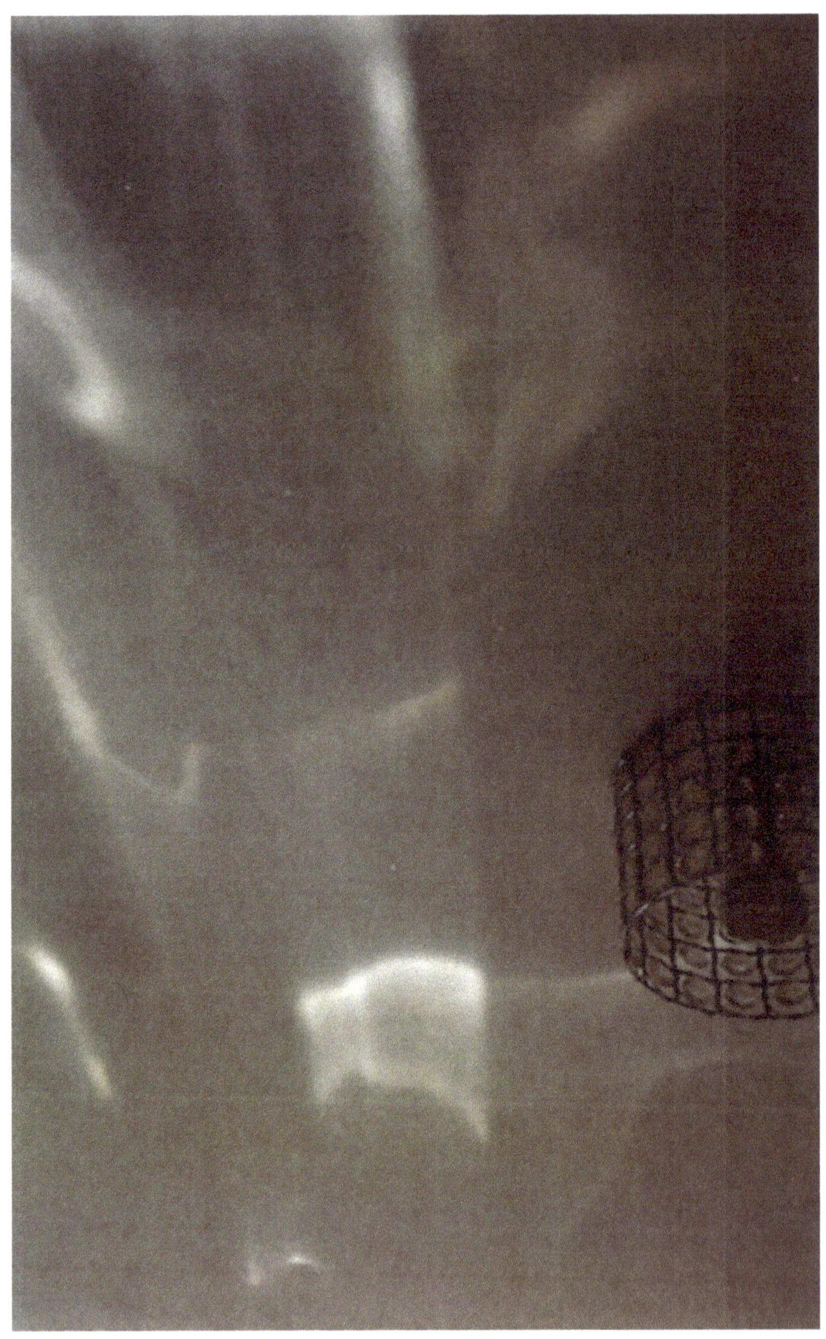

Receiving deeper energy with patterns on our kitchen ceiling with different shapes.

Our friendly spirit has sent me a heart on the wall. A beautiful heart,
I feel so special. Can you see the angelic figure?

The number 7 is divine intervention, the angels are with me
and they show me signs all the time.

Let the peace of this picture fill you with awareness of love from the heavens.

Be open to nature, listen and be still, this is the beautiful angels letting them know they are with me. Open your heart to receive love.

This orb is showing abundance of love and light;
this is when I am called to go outside and walk barefoot
to sit and receive the love and energy.

ABOUT THE AUTHOR

I grew up in the 60's with 3 sisters and 3 brothers. Dad worked as a telephone technician and mum raised the family. We had lots of space to run around and life was very simple back then.

All families have ups and downs, and ours was no different.

As kids, we moved around a lot which made it difficult to settle into any one school. I got married to Gary and we had 3 beautiful boys.

When I was 25 we were living and my six-month old son was asleep, we had no carpet in the hallway of that house. I decided to take a lie down while my son was sleeping. I lay there looking out the window at the beautiful sky, it was around 10am in the morning, all of a sudden I felt a slight pull on my neck and I turned slowly to see a figure in white, it was about 8 feet high with very broad shoulders.

This vision lasted about 30 seconds, once it passed I felt complete peace and serenity. I now know that this was the beginning of my journey with orbs.

After this I started to have vivid dreams which started to come true, I remember this dream, I was signing a document and there was a man in a suit. A month later I saw this house for sale, it was perfect and I had the exact amount to purchase it.

Orbs are very powerful and the energy they use to communicate with me can be intense at times and stop me in my tracks.

They make me feel at peace, yet they invigorate me with their energy. I feel very blessed and special to have been chosen by the angel orbs.

Over the years I have surrendered to this energy more and more and gained more confidence along the way, they came to help me, that I know for sure.

I've come a long way with my life and now with the help of the angel orbs and their powerful energy, I know they are with me all the time and surround me with strength each and every day.

The orbs have communicated to me that they want me to share their beauty and brilliance, they are here to guide us, show us beauty and peace. For years, I have been taking pictures of these beautiful orbs and its now time to share them with you in my first book called "House of Orbs". My wish is for them to communicate to you through my pictures and show you how beautiful they really are and to show you that you have inner beauty as well as on the outside.

ceciliacheck50@gmail.com
www.ceciliaczekanowicz.com.au

Look into the clouds and see the stillness ord wonder of the heavens above.
This is a sure sign that we are being guided and looked after!

www.ingramcontent.com/pod-product-compliance
Lightning Source LLC
Chambersburg PA
CBHW041141300726
48978CB00016B/1343